9th June

To Irene,
My companion along me [...].
thankyou for all adventures
and fun!
May you be blessed with an abundance
of Love, Joy and Prosperity!
Mary xxxx

'Aw Ra Best'

MARY CONNOLLY

BALBOA.PRESS
A DIVISION OF HAY HOUSE

Balboa Press books may be ordered through booksellers or by contacting:

Balboa Press
A Division of Hay House
1663 Liberty Drive
Bloomington, IN 47403
www.balboapress.co.uk
UK TFN: 0800 0148647 (Toll Free inside the UK)
UK Local: 02036 956325 (+44 20 3695 6325 from outside the UK)

Print information available on the last page.

ISBN: 978-1-9822-8349-0 (sc)
ISBN: 978-1-9822-8351-3 (hc)
ISBN: 978-1-9822-8350-6 (e)

Balboa Press rev. date: 05/14/2021

The Beginning

In the beginning was the word, and the word was with Dad, and the word was Dad.

The foundations of family life were based on a strong Catholic, Victorian-influenced background where children should be seen and not heard, and he adhered to a rigid belief in everything the church dictated—including the law on contraception, thus allowing nature to take its course to the tune of thirteen children at the final count, including two sets of twins.

Lucky for some, you might say, but a real pain in the ass for my mother. I'm female and the eldest, and I used to think my siblings were attempts to improve on nature. Perhaps the first production was a disappointment?

There was great emphasis on chapel attendance, twice and sometimes three times on Sundays. One of the more prominent organizations for men was the CYMS (Catholic Young Men's Society), which needed a new label; none of them were any younger than 60 years of age! Communion was a must when we went to Mass. I remember one particular Sunday my sister Cath and I arrived at St Roch's to find the house full and had to sit in the front row. When it came time for communion, members of the congregation got up and made their way to the altar rails—except the Connolly sisters. Why we sat there like a pair of "numpties" I don't know, but after communion was over, the priest returned to the altar and put all the gear away, and at that moment we decided to go to the rails in full view of the congregation. The altar boy drew the priest's attention to the 'pilgrims', and without further ado, he opened the door to the tabernacle, came down the steps, and gave us what we came for. Now you'd think that two shy kids would dream of going into a deserted arena in full view of a packed house, never mind having to make the embarrassing return journey. However, better that than having to face Dad trying to explain something that even we didn't understand.

The church episode reminds me of the story Dad told about his mother, Granny Connolly, who had gone to a late Mass one Sunday and was faced with a dilemma when someone in the congregation farted, and she was torn between leaving her seat and being seen as the culprit or simply fainting, which was the effect bad smells had on her.

Dad's Inventions and Creative Ideas

$$\diamond$$

Dad was interested in many things and had an inventive turn of mind. One day he decided to make butter in the washing machine. This machine would be considered a museum piece nowadays, but back then it was a real luxury. Dad's brother, Uncle John, happened to be selling washing machines at the time, and our rapidly growing numbers made it more of a necessity than a luxury (though I never figured out where the money came from).

It was an upright model, the washing motion alternating in clockwise/anticlockwise movement, swishing the clothes around. I remember him paring slices from an industrial-size bar of cream-coloured soap into the machine, which churned up a lather. An electric wringer, through which the clothes were fed (not necessary for the butter experiment), was attached. Maybe it was the churning motion that gave him the idea for making butter. I watched as he emptied the buttermilk into the churn and started the power, and after what seemed a very long time, blobs began to form on the surface. I don't think it was entirely successful, as the experiment was never repeated, and any ideas of going into the dairy business went down the plughole!

Next came the cream cookies. He was given a recipe for synthetic cream by one of his customers and decided he'd have a go at making cream cookies. I was sent to Ure's Dairy on Royston Road to buy the buns, and when I arrived back, Dad was in the process of making the cream. The buns were cut in half, and cream spread on them like a sandwich. What Dad didn't know was that I had been doing some spreading of my own, having collected a following on my route, resulting in a queue of weans at the door all lined up for free cream cookies. As he handed each bun to me to put on the worktop, I passed them on to the waiting mob. When he realized what was happening, I have a hazy recollection he was, to put it mildly, anything but pleased, though I'm sure later on he saw the funny side.

I can recall a number of incidents featuring my father, like the time my sister, Fran, was about 4 or 5 and recovering from a bout of sickness. She was lying in the top bunk of a two-tier twin cot, which had been moved into what was known as the kitchen (living room to you) so that she'd be in the company of others. I had been asked to give her custard and pears (no problem), except that in order to do this, I had to let down the side of the cot, which opened outwards and would be resting on Dad's bald head while he was dozing peacefully directly underneath. I thought I'd be smart by simply reaching up and passing the plate over the top of the cot rail and into Fran's outstretched hands.

Well, the rest is history, because as I reached up, the plate tilted and the contents fell on Dad, resulting in Fran not getting her just desserts, Dad getting desserts he didn't expect, and me getting desserts I didn't want!

My brother, John (called Johnny back then), was given to temper tantrums and seemed determined to take his revenge on whomever happened to be within reach, and once again Dad was on the receiving end. There he was, having his afternoon nap, lying back, legs stretched out, the newspaper covering his face, and stockinged feet toasting before the fire. Next thing he let out a roar as Johnny sank his teeth into the big toe sticking out of a hole in the sock. Another story starring the same two characters but different props sees Johnny armed with a sweeping brush marching up to a dozing Dad and bringing it down firmly on his bald head.

What more can I say except there must have been times when Dad thought he was on a hitman's list! I'm sure it was his natural sense of humour that saved his sanity.

The "pièce de résistance" for me happened while living in Easterhouse. One evening, while deeply engrossed in thought, I became aware of Dad's voice continually repeating, 'Ma feet's killin' me'. I didn't pay any attention at first, but gradually it began to annoy me, until finally I looked sharply over to where he was seated, back to the window, facing me. My eyes automatically moved down to where I expected his feet to be, and peeping out from beneath the rug he had over his knees were two tiny little boots (they belonged to my brother, Joe, who was a toddler at the time). This totally unexpected sight of Dad's 'shrunken feet' sent me into hysterics, so much so that my mother was on the point of calling the doctor when I ended up rolling round the floor, convulsing with laughter.

The siblings were often used as props for our entertainment. For example, when twins Vera and Betty were about 7 or 8 months old, Cath and I used to lie on the floor, each with a twin seated on our stomachs, and then bounce them up and down, laughing our heads off until we couldn't laugh any more.

Part of our repertoire was to take one small child, one father's jacket, and one chair. One of us would sit on a chair with the tot on the lap. Next step was to turn the jacket back to front, put arms through the sleeves, and wave them frantically about, giving the impression the baby was gesticulating wildly in time to the sound of music.

We didn't have a TV until I was 21 and had moved to a council estate on the outskirts of Glasgow. But who needs a telly when you have your own home-grown entertainment? Sometimes Dad had a laugh at our expense, and once I was sent into Fletcher's newsagents on Royston Road, having been instructed to ask for a packet of "Rollos" in a Cockney accent (Mrs Fletcher originated from London). I was only carrying out orders, but my request was met with a stern gaze as she looked from me to Father, obviously knowing somebody had put me up to it.

He was constantly on the lookout for new and better ways of doing things, and during the war, he bought a Singer electric sewing machine, another wonderful labour-saving device, and in next to no time he set about making patchwork quilts. We were growing up fast as well as in numbers, and I needn't remind anyone about the cost of keeping children in shoes! He bought a shoemaker's last and leather, and when the need arose, he turned cobbler.

There was a large swing park on Royston Road which, apart from being our playground, had another special quality. Our uncle Wullie was in charge of the park, which made us feel very important and safe, as any potential bullies were warned off by the tall, gangly figure of Wullie bearing down on them. He was married to Auntie Minnie, whom I was particularly fond of. Their surname was Kerr, and I remember Cath and me fooling around one day singing out, 'Throw away your Willies and Minnies!' This play on words brought a wee smile to Dad's face.

I am always grateful for my Glasgow roots, particularly the sense of humour, which as the saying goes, like the stick leg, it runs in the family!

What are Willies and Minnies in real life?

Holidays

Every year for a few weeks (sometimes even a month), the city streets were exchanged for a totally different world, where a few times we experienced the luxury of more space, tables with real tablecloths! china cups! shiny cutlery! and of course, food served from another kitchen. This must have been real magic for my mother, away from the daily drudgery of her life in Tharsis Street. I just know that her idea of a *real holiday* would have been away somewhere with no children, no husband, and an opportunity to do exactly as she pleased.

The first holiday I remember was to a place called Strathaven when I was about 6. Mum, Dad, and four children set off in Dad's lorry (which was called Nancy, by the way). The sun shined all the way, the journey made more special with the appearance of chocolate digestives, with milk to follow. On arrival we all tumbled out into what seemed like a paradise of glorious colours and unfamiliar, heady smells. My feet had hardly touched the ground when I took off like a shot, flying over the ground, straight into a huge field full of wildflowers and long grass, where I threw myself down and rolled and rolled until I could roll no more.

Sometimes we went to Co. Tyrone in Ireland and stayed with mum's sister Susan for the whole six weeks of the school holidays.

I have memories of one particular visit when I was 7, because of the number of 'disasters' we managed to create during that period. Brother Johnny (aged 4) decided to take his temper out on a calf roaming around in front of the house by pulling its tail. However, he'd met his match and ended up getting a good sharp kick to teach him a lesson. I was next on the culprit list when I decided to dig a hole at the back of the house. Why? I remember hearing about finding water by digging a well, so I armed myself with a spade and set off to be 'divinely inspired'. I hadn't dug very far when I was discovered and the search for water brought to a halt.

One evening a neighbour called to complain that one of us had rolled in a field of flax and he was going to 'put the summons on us'. I happened to sneak into a room just off the kitchen, where I was able to hear everything as well as peep through a crack in the door. I left poor Cath to face the music (even though she was the culprit so deserved it). I admit to feeling terrified at the prospect of this terrible punishment called 'summons'. I went along to the scene of the crime and stood looking down on a field of beautiful crops waving in the breeze—with a great big dent in it!

My mother was 26 that year, and how she ever managed to travel from Glasgow to Ireland with five children in tow, the youngest being the first set of 10-month-old twins, I can only imagine.

You may wonder where my mother figured in all this (apart from the obvious part she played on the 'production line'). She had a growing resentment at finding herself in an arranged, loveless marriage to a man old enough to be her father, so she simply switched off. This meant going on strike to the extent that she did little or no housework (cooking being the exception) so that Dad had to bring in help a couple times a week.

My father and his brother John came from a fairly well-to-do background with a very comfortable standard of living (grandfather was manager in Brabys local steelworks in Garngad). My mother, on the other hand, was born in Co. Tyrone and left by her parents when she was 3, to be cared for by an assortment of relatives and handed round like a parcel that nobody wanted. Years later she finally admitted she never wanted children and certainly didn't love my father. How could she show love? She'd never been loved and couldn't demonstrate something she hadn't experienced. I found myself in the role of surrogate mother to my siblings, something I bitterly resented as a teenager when I felt deprived of playtime. When I was about 12, I remember quite clearly stating, 'I'm never going to grow up!' Someone pointed out that Mum could have been married to an alcoholic who beat her up. Instead, she was married to a very devout man who worked hard for his family and devoted his life to being mother and father to us. He had to rise early every morning, and drive the lorry down to the fruit market for seven o'clock in Candle Riggs, load up and do the rounds, supplying his customers with fruit and vegetables (none of your GM rubbish then!).

Before he left, he'd had a wee cuppa tea and a smoke after having taken a cup to Mum in bed. Dad was one of the most charitable people you could meet and was continually helping people. Many a time while walking up the street, behind a woman carrying heavy bags of 'messages', he would reach forward and take the load from her, at the same time passing a cheery comment to uplift the spirits. He was the good Samaritan in action, very soft hearted, and I know he loved us all dearly. Sadly, he couldn't show it (his own upbringing strictly forbade any display of emotion).

I have a memory from the past which illustrates this. At 23 I had gone to Dublin to a job which turned out to be totally unsuitable at that time in my life, as I was still recuperating from a breakdown and had just added to my stress by leaving home and going to a place where there was no support. I wrote a letter home expressing how I felt, and Dad replied immediately, urging me to come back to Glasgow.

I don't remember the actual journey back, but on arrival inside the house, I ran straight over to Dad and threw my arms around him, only to feel an invisible barrier, as though he didn't know how to respond. I fled upstairs, only to learn later from one of my sisters that he'd said, 'One of you go up the stairs and see to your sister, Mary; she needs your help'. This was the nearest he could get to showing his love, and I've shed many a tear since, remembering this. Despite our male-dominated upbringing, we have all been blessed with the ability to show unconditional love.

I had to help with various chores: minding siblings, cleaning around the house, and of course 'the messages';the shopping. I ran everywhere and went flying down to McGregor's shop at the corner of Royston Road to buy household cleaners, such as a packet of Rinso for the washing machine. Fletcher's newsagents was just along from 'McGregor's ', and we went there for the Sunday papers: *The People, The Sunday Post,* and *The Empire. The People* fell out of favour when it eventually became too graphic on the taboo subject of sex!

The radio show *Round the Horn*, hosted by Kenneth Horn and Richard Murdoch, was next on the censor's list. It was a real favourite on a Sunday afternoon, and those of us old enough were able to appreciate the double entendre from the cast, especially Kenneth Williams with all the wonderful characters he portrayed, such as Rambling Sid Rumple the gardener, and Jules and Sandy, the gay duo. Father saw all these things as a bad influence on young ears, and the switch off was an attempt to protect us from the evils in the world. It might not have occurred to him that ignorance can create the very problems he wished us to avoid. What on earth would he think of this modern world where anything goes?

Dad and his cousin Dan McCullough (whom we knew as Uncle Dan) had set up the fruit and vegetable business together (McCullough and Connolly) until, sadly, Dan contracted TB and died, leaving his wife, Auntie Sarah, to bring up their five children. Dad took it upon himself to help Dan's family, and every week I was given an envelope containing money to take to Auntie Sarah, who lived at 232 Forge Street. This support continued until their eldest child, James, left school at 14.

Dad supplied fourteen customers (I remember that because I was given the unenviable job of sitting down at his desk every Sunday after Mass, writing out the invoices!—all because I was a 'nice writer'). Actually, my sister Cath and I were chosen as the best writers in our respective classes, and every Friday afternoon we had to parade around the classroom showing our writing to our peers.

There was an amusing incident involving one of his customers, a woman named Carrie Ross who ran a fruit and vegetable shop on Royston Road. The story goes that one of her relatives had come over from a rural area in Ireland for a wee holiday, and Carrie had taken her down to Argyll Street on a shopping trip. At one point Carrie left her outside one of the large stores while Carrie popped inside to make inquiries about something and instructed her to wait outside until she came back, as she would only be a few minutes.

However, the few minutes dragged, and the poor woman, feeling anxious and disorientated with all the noise, hustle and bustle around her, finally turned round to look into the window behind her to find a window dresser putting up a display. She rapped the window sharply and called to the startled figure, 'Hey, sur! Did ya see Carrie Ross?'

This brings to mind another incident concerning a customer, Maggie Carragher, whose shop was in Rosemount Street. One day while delivering goods, Dad came into the shop to find Maggie standing on steps, arms reaching up, arranging items on a shelf. Dad couldn't resist standing behind her and tickling her under the arms. There was a loud report from HQ (hindquarters) as Maggie responded with a massive fart, to the embarrassment of everyone in the shop.

Some of you may remember Joseph Logan's grocery store (next door to Ross's fruit shop). I was sent there every week with 5 pounds, a ration book and the shopping list, which never seemed to change: tea, sugar, butter, eggs, cheese, margarine, cooking fat, chocolate digestive biscuits, things of that sort. My brother, John, recalls a story of how one day Mum sent him to Logan's for some cooked ham. He handed Mr Logan the note for how much he wanted. When Johnny came back and the ham was unwrapped, it was found to have a few extra slices, thanks to the generosity and thoughtfulness of someone who was obviously aware of family life on rations during the war years.

There was always a special effort made at Christmas, and Dad made sure we had a real tree, with lights. Of course, Christmas really was *the* most exciting time of year for us children (just as well, since birthdays were mostly forgotten, and at the rate we were *expanding,* it could turn out to be one a week!). Christmas has become *X-cessmas* in our materialistic, must-have society.

The highlight of festivities was the annual Christmas Eve visit to the circus at Kelvin Hall. Dad always booked a royal box at the side of the ring to accommodate the Connollys.

We arrived in style by taxi, all eight of us, and once inside the hall, a paradise of lights, music, whirling roundabouts, and candy floss surrounded us. We added to the volume with cries of, 'Daddy, Daddy, can we go on the roundabouts, the helter-skelter, the motor bikes, and the dodgems?'

An expensive night out, but Dad believed in celebrating and splashing out on this most special occasion. The wonder of the circus itself, with the dancing horses, the clowns, the highflyers on the trapeze were simply pure magic for us, and the memories and wonder of those times has vividly remained. The evening ended with a taxi ride home and bed for the younger members of the family, while the rest stayed up to attend midnight mass in St Roch's chapel, Royston Road. We were all high as kites, and sleep was the last thing on our minds with the anticipation of Christmas morning and the treasures left by 'Santy Claus'.

However, sleep overcame us eventually until the magic of Christmas morning took over as we discovered our presents. There was always the fried breakfast, where Dad cooked, ham, eggs, sausages, black pudding, and fried pudding (a white, sliced, bread-like roll containing mixed fruit). Dad poured a glass of port, and some of us were allowed to have a wee sip.

Christmas dinner was traditional, with the largest turkey that could be squeezed into the back-to-back oven, having been generously stuffed with Mum's special blend of sage and onion and accompanied by roast potatoes and sprouts (peas and sprouts were named 'musical fruit' by Dad for obvious reasons). The rest of the day was spent playing with our toys, reading the annuals, comics such as Oor Wullie, The Broons, and Tiger Tim.

On one particular Christmas morning during the war (I must have been about 4, Cath a year younger), we jumped out of bed wondering what Santa had brought, only to discover, after much searching, that there were no toys, only an apple and an orange beside the sock we'd hung up the night before. Strangely enough, we didn't even cry but decided we mustn't have been good enough, or even had been very bad not to have received any toys.

It makes me realise the consequences of the messages given to children which can harm how they see themselves in terms of good or bad and result in affecting confidence and self-esteem in later life.

The Church Pipe Band

The Protestant church opposite us in Tharsis Street had a bus trip every summer for the congregation. This was one of the highlights of the year as at the end of the 'day oot', the bus arrived back and deposited the beetroot-faced happy trippers in front of the Kirk around 7.30pm.

That was the cue for the Connollys to take their seats in the royal box (bedroom 'windae' to you) for the evening's entertainment courtesy of the 'kilties'. As you might imagine, they must have been totally knackered after a whole day's piping and drumming but nevertheless treated us all to an extra hour and a half of the best of Scottish, including reels, flings, and a whole array of dashing white sergeants, not to mention encores ending with a rousing rendition of 'Scotland the Brave'.

My love for the pipes and drums stems from those magic moments and still, the stirring sounds of the massed pipe bands creates an emotion like no other.

Uncle John

❖

Uncle John was dad's older brother (approximately eight years between them). He was a multitalented entertainer and practical joker, giving no thought to the one on the receiving end, and we all adored him.

The story goes that when the first wireless set was bought, Granny thought there was a wee man inside (and of course neither John nor Charlie made her any the wiser), and once said to John, 'Och, don't let him into the house, it's not "dacent"'. She wouldn't get undressed while the set was on and insisted on tidying up the room before allowing it to be switched on again.

Another time, when Gracie Fields was 'giving it laldy', Granny said, 'Somebody should put that poor woman out of her misery', whereupon John would march up to the set, switch it off, and at the same time shout, 'Shut up!', leaving poor granny feeling mortified as the last thing she wanted was to offend anyone.

John lived with my parents for a while after they were married, and on one occasion he sent my mother to the chemist in Castle Street to buy a bottle of bronchial cough mixture to clear the tubes (he suffered from chest trouble). It was called Pulmo Bailey, but he instructed her to ask for 'pull ma belly'. Needless to say, the embarrassment this caused my poor mother still in her teens can only be imagined, not to mention the expression on the chemist's face!

John and his wife, Auntie Joan, didn't visit very often, but when they did, we knew it was party time. John would take out his teeth, pretend to swallow them, and then produce them from under his seat.

Another trick was to bring out a little pink linen bag and a white 'dummy' egg. He'd then pop the egg inside the bag, say the magic words, and make the egg disappear. Another highlight of the visit would be heralded by cries of, 'Uncle John, can I comb your hair?' and of course he duly obliged by bending his head while we'd take turns to run a comb through his ample grey locks. It's only now as I write this I realise the novelty this was for us since Dad was completely bald.

I had a particular affection for Uncle John, as he, more than anyone, encouraged me to practice drawing every single day. This spurred me on to be the best that I could be, despite my father's positive/negative mixed message when he'd say, 'You're good, Mary, but you will always meet somebody better than yourself'. Comments like that were meant to keep me from getting big headed, although they could have had the opposite effect by making me feel that I wasn't *good enough,* and that is why I was so lucky in those early years to have my uncle John's encouragement to continually practice drawing every single day.

Childhood Memories

I was born at 20 Tharsis Street, Garngad, Glasgow, on 1 March 1937, a few months before my mother's 19th birthday.

My first memory at 3 years old was of standing alongside my 2-year-old sister Cathy in front of a completely empty cupboard (except for a banana), which my mother took out, cut in half, and gave a piece to each of us. Looking back on that far-off memory, it's kind of symbolic as war had just begun, and that memory represented a symbol of moving from a life of relative abundance to one of rationing, coupons, gasmasks, and blackouts.

This was the world in which we grew up.

One thing I found totally unacceptable was the gasmask. They came in square cardboard boxes and were referred to as Mickey Mouse (this supposedly was an attempt to create a friendly image to take away the real look), which was more like something from a horror movie. The sensation of being smothered was enough for me, and I immediately pulled it off my face! Thankfully, we never had the occasion to wear them.

I started school round about this time, and I remember standing in line in a very long, white, tiled corridor holding my mother's hand as we waited to be enrolled in Our Lady and St Francis Convent school, Charlotte Street.

I was more than a little apprehensive with this new experience, especially when standing before the headmistress, Mother Mary Phillipa, a pale-faced woman with a grim expression, framed in a white starch, 'surround' topped off with a black veil and ending in a long black dress. She was headmistress for my eleven years as a pupil.

The school was situated beside Glasgow Green in the Gorbals area.

The uniform was a brown gym slip, blue tie, cream blouse, brown trench coat, and a hat. I even had a pair of little cream-coloured kid gloves! How my father ever managed to get together enough money for the uniform, never mind kid gloves, I'll never know, since it was wartime (1942), rationing on all fronts and a growing family to bring up. Every morning I was put on the bus clutching my little brown case containing some jotters, pencils, and a piece of cold buttered toast wrapped in paper for the break at playtime.

Don't remember much about the first year except that I was given the prize for general excellence (whoever the real winner was didn't turn up, so I got the prize!!). I can still remember the beautifully illustrated book with two wise sayings: 'Pride cometh before a fall' and 'The watched pot never boils'. Ours was the only class in the school with boys, seven of them. They made their presence felt the way little boys do, and after two years they were no longer on the roll call. I still remember some of them: Ronald Ponsonby, Terence Burke, Billy McCann, James Maguire, and Gary (whose last name I forget).

I can't honestly say I liked school; I felt shy and uncomfortable and experienced the same butterflies in my stomach every morning on my way there, and to a large extent that feeling has never left.

I made my first communion aged 7, and my parents must have made sacrifices to prepare me for this special day with all its religious significance. I was taken to a dressmaker to be measured for a dress. The day of the fitting arrived, and I tried on the long white satin dress with a Peter Pan collar. To complete the outfit were a pair of silver shoes, a veil, and a little circlet of white flowers.

When the big day arrived, no expense was spared as I stepped into a taxi accompanied by Mum and Auntie Joan (Uncle John's wife), and then we sped off to Merrylee Convent in Giffnock, where I met up with all my classmates, teachers, and nuns to help celebrate. After the Mass, we were ushered into a big room set for breakfast. Afterwards I was taken to Jerome's photographer in Argyle Street to have the obligatory 'foty' (otherwise known as a phtotograph)for posterity!.

The radio was our entertainment box, and I hurried home every day and made straight for the wireless in the corner to listen to *Auntie Kathleen presenting 'Children's Hour'*, with tales of Tammy Troot and a host of favourites. The evening highlights were episodes of *Dick Barton, Special Agent*, or *Journey into Space*. What a treat for the imagination where you really lived in another magic world.

There was a mass campaign to target diphtheria, which meant an unpleasant trip to the local school to have our jabs. I stood in line, dreading the moment and crying loudly after 'the attack', with Dad trying to pacify me with a 'sweetie' and the promised visit to the pictures. We took the bus to the city centre and went straight to Green's Playhouse, where it was up in a lift to 'the gods' with the darkness adding to the mystery. Dad made sure we went to the toilet, and then the first sight of the big screen and a giant Bob Hope with lots of ladies prancing around in what appeared to be feathers was so overwhelming. I screamed, 'Oh, look at the big man!' and a stage whispered, 'Be quiet!' followed from dad.

That first introduction to the big screen was the beginning of a lifelong love of the cinema. My particular favourites were the Hollywood musicals in glorious black and white. I always went through a personality change afterwards for a short time until the next movie visit. I came out with my head buzzing to the magic of Fred Astaire and Ginger Rodgers's dancing feet and wanted more than anything to have a pair of tap shoes so I could dance everywhere! One of my favourite classes at school was Scottish country dancing with Miss Kelly. We had the use of the TA (territorial army hall) situated in a little side street behind the school, and twice a week we trooped over clutching our gym shoes. I remember during one class how thrilled I was when she remarked as I passed, 'Beautiful feet'.

Dancing didn't stop after class, oh no! For a magic half hour, I flew around the kitchen in Tharsis Street to the music of Jimmy Shand and his band, broadcast a couple times a week around 7.30 pm.! I knew somewhere deep inside I had the ability to dance, sing, and generally entertain, but so often, when in full flight, the words, 'Stop acting the goat, Mary', had the effect of making me feel as though I was doing something wrong.

Going to the pictures was the highlight of our week, and most Saturday mornings, those of us old enough set off along Royston

Road to the matinee at the Carlton Cinema in Castle Street for a dose of escapism where we entered into the comedy world of Charlie Chaplin, Laurel and Hardy, or Abbot and Costello one week. On the next visit we might be transported to the land of cowboys and Indians riding alongside John Wayne conquering the Wild West. One particular Saturday we were each handed a brand-new chocolate bar just arrived on the market, called Kit Kat, as a special treat!

The Burns family lived below us, and Mrs Burns must have had the patience of a saint as I never remember any complaints about the racket—though every Saturday night you could say they got even when the week's worries were set aside and it was party time, where they all got 'fu' and 'gave it laldy' (create an uproar) and the world was transformed.

Dad was fond of telling the story about the time Mrs Burns and her daughter, Margaret, called one evening, and during the course of the visit, wee Margaret was squirming around on her chair, until she eventually announced, 'Ma, ah've nae knickers oan!' Nothing extraordinary about that you might think—except that she was sitting on Granny's horsehair chair!

Mrs McDermott, referred to as Mrs Mac, was called upon from time to time by my father to 'change the "current" baby's nappy since my mother had gone shopping. She was the ideal neighbour in many ways practical and a regular good Samaritan.

One day, when my sister, Cath, and I were in bed (probably to have a nap and give my mother some peace!), I went into the bathroom, found a box of matches, brought them back to the room, sat on the bed beside the sleeping Cath, and began to strike the matches, lying one on the quilt before striking another. Very soon there was a nice little blaze going.

My next move was to run into the scullery and tell my mum, 'There's a wee fire in the room'. Next minute Mum rushed into the room and grabbed Cath out of the line of fire.

Mrs Mac then dashed in, set about putting out the flames, and immersed the smoking covers in a sink full of water. All I was concerned about was the fact that the 'darkie doll' (very non-pc) I had received for Christmas was covered in blisters, which I began to pop one by one, ending up with a polka dot dolly.

Dad's gift for storytelling had us all enthralled on many evenings, and it was only years later we learned that the stories were his own creations and he spent the customers rounds each day wracking his brains to come up with the next episode! I took over as bedtime storyteller at some point, and it gave me the opportunity to use my love of entertaining, creating characters and voices to match the particular story. The favourite among these was the 'Brer Rabbit' tales, by Enid Blyton, and I still remember seeing my brothers and sisters' enthralled expressions as they were transported to that magic land of make believe until sleep eventually overcame them and all was quiet.

The War Game (1917), Charles A. Connolly (1898–1969)

'If you're livin', for God's sake, write'. These words were written in a letter I received from my mother in Glasgow a short time ago. And so begins his journal …

There are no words to describe the horrors of war, but what happened the other day summed up the futility of it all. I was in a trench near the front line when orders came to prepare for an advancing enemy attack. How much preparation can you make in such a situation when faced with the real possibility of death? A time to pray, indeed, and even those who have never said a prayer in their lives have been crying to God for help.

I crouched down in the dugout as the advancing sounds of 'Gerry' grew louder, until, next minute I was literally bowled over by a sudden weight falling on top of me. I thought I was sent for. I lay there stunned till the survival instinct kicked in, and I raised my head to see what had hit me and found myself looking into the eyes of a German soldier. He couldn't have been any more than 16, just a wee boy crying for his mammy. In between sobs he was pointing to his leg, which I could see was covered in blood with a big piece of shrapnel sticking out. I patted him on the shoulder and told him he'd be all right, hoping he'd at least understand my desire to help him. There is no language barrier in such a situation.

I brought out the first aid kit we all carried. The shrapnel hadn't gone in too deep, and it was a matter of cleaning the wound as best I could and then applying a bandage. As I worked away, my German comrade began to speak through the tears, pulling out photos of his mother and father, pointing at each one to help me understand. Here I was, Charlie Connolly, 19 years old, from the Garngad in Glasgow, lying in a mucky trench in France, sharing the space with a wee German laddie, while we looked at his photos, tears streamin' down our faces.

When I'd finished dressing the wound, I waited till there was a lull in the firing before sending him off with a prayer, a couple of fags, and some chocolate. I buried my head in my hands, as in that moment I realized that could have been me hoping for a good Samaritan. I cried.

One aspect of human nature tends to be forgotten in these times, and that is a sense of humour essential for survival. A wee while ago, somebody came up with the idea of playing a joke on one of our boys. Now, nobody knows how Tony was accepted for the army, since he's stone deaf. I suppose it had got to the stage if you had all the necessary limbs, you'd do. Anyway, the plan was that at a given signal we'd all pretend there was an imminent air raid attack, crouch down, and wait. Tony of course kept his eyes glued to our every move, mirroring everything we did. Unknown to him, there was somebody behind him with a pile of stones in a tin helmet (we all wore these).

The signal rang out 'Fire!' and as the contents of the tin hat fell on Tony, he yelled out, 'Jesus Christ, I've been hit!'

A joke at Tony's expense, but he took it in good part, seeing the funny side.

I haven't had a chance to write anything for a few weeks as things have got worse. We've had very little sleep; it's turned extremely cold, freezin', in fact, real brass monkey weather. Some of us have been billeted in a barn adjoining a farmhouse, where a young woman and her two wee girls lived. Her husband was in the army, and any communication had to be done through pantomiming as none of us knew any French, except maybe basic stuff. I had learned some French at school, but apart from '*la plume d e ma tante et sur le bureau de mon oncle*', and the like, I had only retained a couple of sentences from *The Three Bears*. One time the French teacher came in, and a few jokers greeted him with, 'Bonjour, manure' (you could say that went down like a shit sandwich!).

Our present situation called for more basic requirements, like food and shelter. The woman didn't have much, but she brought some blankets which, along with the hay in the barn, we managed to make ourselves comfortable while awaiting further orders to march. She even brought some coffee and tea, and we shared our chocolate rations in return.

She usually arrived in the early evening accompanied by the wee ones.

One evening I noticed only one of the girls was with her. Through a series of gestures, it turned out the other one was sick and had to stay in bed. Then I had a thought that maybe a wee bedtime story would help. I didn't think for a moment what I might be letting myself in for.

So next thing, I grabbed my notebook, opened it, and kept repeating, '*Il etait une fois*' (once upon a time), while pointing to the little girl. Magically, the woman seemed to understand and nodded enthusiastically, delighted at the idea.

The three of us set off into the house and up the stairs to where the wee girls slept. The child was lying back but sat up as we entered the room. I remember voicing some kind of greeting, gesticulating at the same time (always a safe bet in France, as I heard someone say, if they had their hands cut off, they'd be speechless!), and hoping she'd understand. Mama explained that I was going to tell a bedtime story and the wee face lit up, and she gave me the nicest smile. I sat at the bottom of the bed while the big sister knelt at my feet with bated breath awaiting this wonderful story.

And so I began, managed three or four lines, and then my French ran out! Try as I might, I just couldn't continue, and the wee faces changed from wide-eyed anticipation to loud wails of disappointment. In the midst of all this, the mother appeared to find a vacant looking 'storyteller' perched on the edge of the bed, her two daughters in floods of tears. I knew it was fruitless, my attempting to explain what happened, but gradually through their intermittent sobs, the whole sorry tale emerged and ended in smiles when I fished out some chocolate from my pocket.

It's been a week of heavy fighting, and a couple of times, I felt sure I was about to meet my Maker. Some light relief came in the form of a food hamper for one of our lads, the Welshman nicknamed Taffy. It seemed a miracle it had arrived intact. It was packed full of wonderful Welsh produce, and we were all gathered round this mouth-watering treasure. Taffy announced that this hamper wasn't just for him, it was for all of us. But before we could even sample any of the contents, a massive burst of enemy fire brought us back to reality. Orders came for us to move quickly, some fifty yards, to the relative safety of a building opposite. The procedure was to wait for a short lull between each blast before making a run for it. Taffy was last in line (his choice). He held the precious hamper close to his chest, and as we watched, breathless after our dash, Taffy made his courageous bid for safety, only to be blown to smithereens right before our eyes; bits of him everywhere mixed in with the contents of the precious hamper, packed with so much love and care.

I know in that moment I made a solemn vow that if God spares me to return home safely, I would search till I found the biggest pictures of the Sacred Heart and his Holy Mother in thanksgiving. I'm nearly 20 now and prayer was, until now, reserved for chapel attendance on Sundays, trotted out in parrot fashion, like reciting the ten times table. Now each morning on waking I give thanks I'm still here.

Things have been quiet for almost a week now, thanks be to God, and there's rumours going round that the war could be over soon, but I wouldn't bet on it. The other day one of the lads asked if I could give him a hand to do something. He'd developed a severe case of impetigo but didn't report it, thinking it would clear up. His whole face was a scab mask, and he'd got to the stage where he could hardly eat or drink, never mind shave. The doc had diagnosed the problem and gave him a big box of ointment with instructions to remove all the scabs before applying it. That's where I came in, because he asked me to hold a mirror in front of him. I felt sick at the sight of an open razor slicing through unsightly scabs as the blood poured down his face. I could hardly keep my hand steady, and the solution was to focus intently on my hands and avoid raising my eyes to the bloody mess. At last the gristly operation was finished and the ointment applied, leaving me to check up on the whereabouts of my stomach.

Life wasn't without its lighter moments, as there was an announcement that Field Marshall Alexander was paying a visit to the regiment in a few weeks' time and orders went out to make sure we put in an extra effort for his benefit. The high ranking bigwig was well known as an athletics champion, especially in sprinting. Meanwhile, a few of the lads had got together with a plan to bring some light relief into our lives involving a wee bit of sport. The plan was to dress one of our lads in a female soldier's uniform to stand beside him while he was having some refreshment, pinch his cap, and run! Like all the rest, I could envisage the fun this would create—that was until I discovered I'd been chosen as the female!

I was the smallest in the regiment, so it seemed logical to pick somebody who'd fit the uniform. I don't know how they managed to get the uniform, including hat, a wig, and even lipstick, but I can tell you that was the least of my thoughts.

The stage was set and a message sent round that the VIP would be inspecting the Mess on the afternoon of the third day of his visit. Yours truly was hastily transformed into a female soldier, everything going to plan, except that I had an attack of stage fright and persuaded the lads to let me have a wee snifter to calm the nerves. I decided another wee snifter wouldn't go amiss and made that a double, until I could hardly walk, never mind run!

I caught sight of myself in a mirror in the 'dressing room' and the hazy reflection of an odd looking 'female', with a hat that didn't know which way to turn, a hair 'do' that didn't, and a very blotchy red face. And so ended my acting career, the performance cancelled, and I was hurriedly ushered offstage to the relief of all concerned.

The war finally came to an end, but not before I was wounded in the leg and packed off to 'blighty'. This was a blessing in disguise, and before returning home I found myself in the FUN (far upper north) ward at the military hospital.

To be continued …

How to 'Patch' up Your Troubles and Address Life through Vitality!

❖

An evening with Patch Adams MD (doctor of 'mirth and medicine', portrayed by Robin Williams in the movie that bore the doctor's name) certainly proved to be quite an experience from the word go. The appearance of his tall lanky frame, wearing a dolly mixture t-shirt, headed by waist-length grey hair tied back in a ponytail, and sporting a most impressive handlebar moustache, was an instant reminder of a cross between Don Quixote and Salvador Dali. One could almost apply the term artistic eccentric to his vibrant approach to humour and therapy. He informed us that although he is a qualified doctor, his career in clowning has been long established for some thirty years or so. Having a laugh is not simply a range of muscles coming into play in response to a punch line, or something which tickles your particular sense of humour. It could be described as beneficial, as it can dramatically transform the wearer, as well as give a lift to the spirit.

Dr Adams discussed the connection between humour and wellness by stating that, 'Wellness is good health with the absence of disease', and he urges us to celebrate the gift of being alive,— which makes me question the origins of remarks such as 'You're dead lucky!' or 'That's dead brilliant!' He drew our attention to the connection between humour and play, with its wonder, curiosity, passion, hope, wisdom, and creativity, to serve as a reminder that the spirit is free and the quality of surrender to the spirit is seen in the wonder and curiosity of children.

His hand-in-hand description of play and humour certainly gives a more street-level understanding of the relationship between the two, when compared with this quotation I came across recently describing play: 'A state of engagement in which the successive nonliteral behaviours of one partner are contingent on the nonliteral behaviours of the other partner'! Well that doesn't sound like much fun, does it?

He described loneliness as the worst disease, in line with fear and boredom, and it is labelled as a medical emergency, medically defined as 'psychoimnoneuroimmunology'!

He went on to say, 'Why is it, when depression and disease strike, we say, "I will play music, dance, sing, have a party, get totally pissed, take up a new hobby—when I feel better"?'

Does that ring a bell? Yes, that's definitely me, as it fits his definition of depression as, 'A lack of capacity for responsiveness'.

He urged us to, 'Find your own joy and insist in being it! It's easy to have a bad day, and if you want a lousy day, you'll easily find it by waking up!'

He told us that the most revolutionary act committed today is to be publicly happy, stating that, 'Pessimism is a learned behaviour, as no adult looks as if they're enjoying themselves'.

Dr Adams was no naive exponent of the 'Pollyanna' philosophy, as much of what he said makes sense; although I think a number of people would draw the line at his sporting a pair of wings and a harp, waltzing into a ward, and announcing to a patient, 'Here are the forthcoming attractions!' Perhaps an appropriate response to that might be, 'Gee, Doc, I was just dying to hear you say that!' (One might have to weigh the consequences between humour and therapy here.)

His account of a visit to the bank manager was a typical illustration of his extroverted sense of the ridiculous, when he arrived, suitably attired in a three-piece suit, with matching accessories, and ... a pair of Y fronts (a type of underwear) on his head! I defy anyone to keep a straight face confronted by such an image.

Another side to Dr Adams shows a caring, sensitive human being engaged in working tirelessly for the good of humanity. He has visited Russia on a number of occasions and is currently engaged in gathering funds and co-workers to build a hospital where, as well as practising his medical skills, patients will find themselves being prescribed suitable doses of humour therapy (funnily enough!).

'Well, Mr Moses, my diagnosis shows us you are still alive and not dead. Forget the two tablets—I'll give you commandments: go out and "get stoned" instead!'

'Well Mr. Moses,
My diagnosis showeus,
You are still alive and not dead,
Forget the 2 tablets,
I'll give you Commaindments,
Go out and 'get stoned' instead.'

ILLUS. for article on 'Dr. Patch Adams'

Coincidences or God Instances

———————— ✧ ————————

While living in Edinburgh, I began to notice coins lying in the street. Now you could say, 'That's not so unusual'. I never looked for them intentionally, and it seemed that on these occasions my eyes would suddenly look down and there it would be. I'd pick it up and, as is the custom where I come from, pass it on to the next person I would meet to 'share the luck' (provided they didn't misinterpret the intentions, when the 'lucky' recipient happened to be a tourist and not terribly familiar with English!). It became a joke among my friends, who began to ask how much I'd made on the streets recently!

I remember one frosty New Year's morning, I left the house to go to botanics, and a small silver disc caught my eye just as I stepped out onto the street. It turned out to be a silver three-penny piece. This was a very unusual find since these coins had been phased out many years before. I popped it into my pocket and continued on my way. On my return, just a short distance from where I discovered the first coin, didn't I spy another one! I looked on the discovery as a very lucky omen and hurried upstairs to examine them. One had Queen Victoria's image and dated 1896. The other was more worn, dated 1914 with the head of then king George quite visible.

Now, I have to mention that since my father's death in 1969, I have experienced signs of his presence on quite a few occasions. Finding the coins was one of these. There is always a message within the signs or symbols. The one dated 1896 was just two years before my father was born, and the other was the date of the First World War, in which my father served for a year when he was 19.

As I mentioned earlier, it was a cold, frosty morning, and as I stood with my back to the fire holding the 1914 piece in my hand I simply couldn't get warm, and it was only years later that I came to understand the meaning of the message. One evening, on my way back to the flat, I saw two people a short distance ahead of me. One was tall, the other much smaller. As I drew level with them I recognized the small, elderly figure as Mr Baxter, my neighbour from downstairs. He was obviously in a distressed state (he had started drinking shortly after his wife died a few months before), and the young man with him explained that he had fallen in the bar where he happened to be and was taking him home. We were only a short distance from the flat, and I suggested I take over and see him safely upstairs.

However, Mr B. was a very independent man and wouldn't accept any further help, and all I could do was thank the kind Samaritan and go up to my own flat. I come to the 'God instance' of this story. After saying good night to my son, Paul, who was staying with me at the time, I went to bed and picked up the book (by the Dalai Lama) I was currently reading. I opened a page at random and began to read words to the effect, 'You may see, ahead of you, an elderly person who is in need of help'.

You can guess my amazement at these words. I immediately jumped out of bed, called my son, and we both looked over the railings to see my neighbour lying face down on the ground floor. We managed to get him upstairs and into his bed, and he kept saying, 'But how did you know?' Explanations unnecessary.

Like other people, I have experienced déjà vu, and one that comes to mind concerns my son. One morning on my way to the shop, I saw Paul at the far end of the road, walking towards me. However, when I looked down the road again, he was no longer there, and I assumed he'd gone into one of the shops on the way. I assumed he had called into the supermarket on the way past, but when I looked again, he was walking down the road exactly as I had seen him only seconds before.

The new (or not so new) language is composed of synchronicity, coincidences, symbols, signs, and other things we tend to use when describing something we cannot explain in 'learned language'. I began to take an interest in coincidences when I started to notice patterns in various situations in my life.

There appeared to be a sort of code and repeat pattern in incidents which, when observed and followed through, lead to solving a problem, contacting someone, or learning something. For instance, Sylvia, a friend whom I hadn't been in touch with for some time, came into my mind, and then a few days later while I was looking for something among a pile of photos, a photo of the same friend fell out of an album. I tried to stick it back again without success and put it to one side, intending to insert it later.

Next morning, when I switched on the radio, the song being played, was 'Sylvia Where Are You'? I remembered thinking, 'I must give her a ring', but of course, day-to-day life takes over, and it wasn't until a week or so later, while listening to songs on the radio, once again, the same song was repeated. This gave me the much-needed jolt to get in touch, and it was only then, during our conversation, the reason for the prompts became clear. I have found out through these experiences that this is a definite form of communication which uses ESP and other dimensions to bring about contact between people *through modern technology*.

Some years ago, while on a counselling course in Edinburgh, I experienced an instance of 'spirit communication' through the word processor. I was working on an essay, and one line in the text suddenly said, 'You have a blockage', and it changed from black to red and moved 'out of line'. I wasn't aware of doing anything to cause this, but afterwards, when I was checking the essay, the meaning of 'message' became clear (revealing the blocked energies in the chakras).

Most of us have asked the question, 'Why am I here?' One day I was feeling totally lost, frustrated, and generally pissed off with any god within spitting distance as to why I never seemed to get a satisfactory answer to these questions. So I went into Bewley's Tearoom in Edinburgh, sat down, took out the pen and pad, and wrote a very respectful, but 'in your face', letter to God in which I once again asked, 'Which path do I follow? Is it through my artistic talents or healing therapy?' I ended with a heartfelt plea for an immediate answer.

That evening, the phone rang and I found myself talking to a woman who had seen some of my work in the window of a shop in Edinburgh. She knew the owner, who gave her my phone number, and when she contacted me, she asked if I'd be interested in doing a portrait of her two dogs. She mention that sadly, one of the dogs had died a few years ago, but she could supply me with a good selection of photographs. I was invited to come along and meet Jennifer, the remaining St Bernard, and I thought, 'This could be my *biggest* commission yet!' This goes to prove that God is listening, and answers letters.

Another friend, Laura, popped into my mind one day, and once again, the medium (no pun intended) came via radio. I found myself listening to 'Laura' being sung in French, which happened twice within a week, and when I acted on it, not only had she been thinking about me, but there was a clear message why I'd got in touch. When I rang her, I discovered her father had just died.

My experiences of this 'new' communication is that the messages tend to come in threes, but sometimes it only takes two. I'll give you an example. Recently while on a visit to Valencia, I noticed one of my earrings was causing discomfort. I put up with it for a day, thinking that by tomorrow it would have settled down. However, it was exactly the same, so I decided to remove it. Later, while waiting for a bus to go back to the friend's flat where I was staying, I happened to gaze at a large poster on the side of the building opposite. I had noticed it before, but as I stood, my eyes moved to the text at the top, which translated said 'Give wings to your voice'. I immediately felt a strong sense of knowing that those words were for me, and I saw all the connections leading to this moment. The poster showed two men sitting side-by-side wearing wings. Things become clearer when I tell you that the earring was in the shape of a pair of wings fastened together. The message meant I hadn't been listening to my inner voice and had to be given very direct orders, in which the events happened were exactly right to draw my attention to the fact that I wasn't focusing on my life's purpose.

Once, while on the train traveling to Beziers from a day out in Narbonne, I was listening to my CD player and happened to notice a woman opposite looking very intently in my direction. I smiled, stopped listening to the music, and we began to exchange a few words. She was admiring the earphones, which incidentally were held together with Sellotape at one point but were still fully functional.

She sadly couldn't listen to her music because her earphones were broken. Within the next few minutes, I made the decision to give her the earphones, so, on arrival at Beziers, I got up and handed them to an astonished and delighted lady.

The story doesn't end there, because some months later, while traveling from San Sebastian to Beziers by bus (this is an eight-hour overnight journey), I had a very unexpected surprise next morning as the day dawned. I gazed at the back of the seat in front, and there in the pocket I saw what I took to be a cord hanging down. I pulled it gently and ... out came a pair of earphones! I said thank you—of course.

I know the theory that letting go often creates a boomerang effect, and I'll tell you of my experiences with this. I had a jacket with a belt which loosely hung at the side. One morning I picked up the jacket to go out and noticed the belt was missing. I had a quick look round the room and decided that it had probably dropped out on the street the day before. A few days later, I went to the market in Puisserguier and while standing at one of the stalls, a woman I knew from Creissan came up to me and said she had found my missing belt and said it was tied to a railing near her house. Later, on my way back from the market, I had a good look along the way but still no sign of the belt.

I then realised I had never used it anyway and let it go. Some days later, while walking in the village, I spied the belt tied to a drainpipe! One of the most surprising happenings to date.

I decided to go to Narbonne (market day). I had a wonderful time, and when I decided to return to Beziers, there was approximately a forty-five minute wait for the train. There were two bars across from the station, and I went into one and sat with a coffee until it was time to catch the train. After the coffee, I crossed the road and went into the station, found a seat, and sat back to enjoy the short trip back to Beziers.

Feeling relaxed after my day out, I looked for my bag to check something when I discovered the bag wasn't there! Strangely enough I didn't panic, simply sat still, until I realized I'd left it on the hook behind the toilet door in the bar. This bag contained all my credit cards, plus cards relating to my being a resident in France, as well as a little money.

I had thoughts of getting off the train and going back to the bar but dismissed this idea as being impractical. A better thought was to find the ticket inspector. I told him my tale and he advised me to go straight to Information on arrival in Beziers. Normally there is never anyone in the info booth, but that day I was in luck and spoke to the lady on duty. You'd think she was primed for handling emergencies, as almost before I had finished my story, quick as a flash, she had the phone directory out and asked me the name of the bar.

I didn't know the name but she guessed it was 'such and such' (in French of course!), and next thing I knew, she was through to the bar in Narbonne explaining the situation. But back came the reply, 'Sorry, no bag here'. She then left the booth, locked up, and ushered me into the station control room where two men were working in front of computers. A few more questions for me (such as bank details), and she was off again, this time to have my credit cards cancelled.

I was told I had to report theft to the police in Capestang. I was in Beziers with no means of getting there (no bus service and I didn't have a car). Then I remembered a friend from the same village, and rang to find John at home. When I explained the situation, he immediately drove to Beziers, picked me up, and then on to the police station in Capestang where I gave a report on the 'theft'. Afterwards I did all the necessary reporting, cancelling, and reordering new cards and got on with life.

Some months later, two friends invited me to a girls day out in Narbonne. It was always a fun day where we had coffee and croissants, a browse around the market, lunch in a favourite restaurant, and then back to the village.

That particular day, while waiting at the lights across from the station, I looked over at the bar where I had left the bag months before, and suddenly realised that my kind Samaritan at the station had rung the wrong bar! I asked Susan if she could possibly pull into the station and wait while I crossed the road to the bar. As I walked towards the counter, the barman recognised me, reached up to a shelf above him, and produced the bag.

All the cards were there exactly as I left them (no cash of course). Just another instance of letting go and magic happens.

My Double Life

❖

I've come to the conclusion that I have a very common face, as everywhere I go people seem to think they know me. Even here, in the south of France, where I've been living for the past three years, I have the same experience, so now I just tell myself I'm famous! Once, while chatting with a woman in an Edinburgh loo, the attendant, who was busily engaged in her work, must have been listening to the conversation, because she stopped, turned to me, and inquired if I was on TV.

I replied, 'I used to be, but I had to give it up as I kept falling off'. She seemed satisfied with this and continued with her work.

I had a similar experience many years ago while living in the north of Spain. The family were going on holiday, and we stopped in Logrono to buy something in a chemist shop. I took the children inside and we stood waiting to be served.

The assistant looked at me and the boys and then exclaimed, 'My, what a surprise! I haven't seen you for ages, and how the boys have grown!'

This took me completely by surprise as you can imagine and was the cause of much eyebrow raising and wonderment when I explained that not only was this the first time we had ever visited that part of the country, I was a foreigner!

Also during the same holiday, I decided to do some sightseeing in the little village and found myself outside an old church. Isn't it interesting that whether a church is in the country or the city, as soon as you step inside there is an air of tranquillity to give the soul a breathing space? I sat for a while and found my eyes resting on some votive candles near the altar, and feeling a sense of peace and connection with all sentient beings, I decided to go and light up and then leave to join the rest of the family for the evening meal.

Next day being Sunday and still in pious mode, I set off for the church to attend Mass. My pious intentions faded somewhat as the priest began his sermon and *the collective unconscious,* or *sermonitis,* took over. The symptoms usually include yawning, nodding off, and even keeling over. However, not wanting to embarrass myself, I made an effort to pay attention and see how much Spanish I could understand (we'd been living in the country for two years at that time), when suddenly, something made me really sit up and take notice. I became aware that my visit to the church the evening before was the subject of the sermon!

The pastor was drawing the attention of the congregation to the sad fact that no one thinks of coming to pay a visit to La Virgen de Albelda (name of the church)—that was, all except one, who came alone, to pay homage to La Virgen yesterday. I felt quite touched and at the same time amused, as I pictured the poor man racking his brains, praying for miraculous inspiration in an effort to come up with a subject for next day's sermon! Ask and you shall receive, but be careful what you ask for!

While we are discussing Spain, I may as well tell you about

the time I became a magician's assistant. I was spending a winter in the south of Spain at the time, and a woman, called Dorita, whom I had befriended, invited me to go to a show in one of the hotels nearby. She didn't hide the fact that she was man hunting.

On that particular evening I was more interested in having a night in, but I gave in to the prospect of a boring old sit-down just to please her. It started off as I had expected, with me parked at a table drinking something alcoholic, hoping to 'raise the spirits' and stave off the boredom I had anticipated. That was, until the magic happened in the form of a real magician. Yes, there he stood, complete with colourful robes, sparkles everywhere, even down to his 'curly' shoes.

After producing a few items out of mid-air, he began to survey the audience, and next thing I realised I was being escorted from my seat and led out to stand under the spotlight and have my fifteen minutes of fame as a magician's assistant! After the applause died down, he produced the most beautiful pink fan you could imagine; it was enormous, all fluffy feathers, glittering under the spotlights. He handed it to me, and suddenly it collapsed into a bedraggled mass! I gasped and stood there with my mouth open, waiting for the next set of instructions after the laughter settled down. He pulled a string of chiffon scarfs from thin air and then stood behind me and told me to keep perfectly still. I felt some movement on my back and 'Presto!' I looked up to see him holding aloft the biggest bra I'd ever seen in my life!

My reaction was to say, 'That is real magic, since I'm not even wearing one!' My fifteen minutes over, I made my way back to my seat and Dorita, who looked at me as though I'd had a personality change. As I passed one table, a man leaned over and asked me if he'd seen me at the summer season in Eastbourne (or somewhere like that).

Here's a typical example of my lookalike experiences. One day while walking along a street in Edinburgh, a woman stopped me and started chatting, asking me how I was, how was the family, things of that sort. I had never met the woman in my life, yet always in those circumstances I just pretend that we know each other and carry on chatting.

At one point, she suddenly stopped, an embarrassed look came over her, and she began to apologise profusely at having mistaken me for someone else. I told her I thoroughly enjoyed our conversation, and she could apparently see the funny side. We parted like old friends with a story to tell.

Life in Creissan, France

Francophile, July 2007

There is an unreal quality about village life for me, and I once heard someone liken French villages to ghost towns, though after nearly four years living in one, I have to disagree. The first impression for the visitor is the quaint, old-world atmosphere and the slow pace of life (ideal for a relaxing holiday). Before moving here, I lived in a flat in the middle of Edinburgh and can honestly say it was quieter.

Perhaps it's because I happen to be in a street where the noisiest people in the village live. Eric and Françoise don't talk to each other, they yell. They have two children, four dogs, cats, and a variety of other assorted pets that fly or swim depending on whether they have fins or feathers. The amazing thing is, you'd never know, because you never hear *them*! That is, all except a recent addition to the household, in the form of a very skinny little black dog which has the exact same voice quality as Françoise. Difficult to describe, except that they both yap in top C. I realised this one day when I couldn't tell one from the other! Add to that competition from 'motos' that go careering along the roads, and there you have it in a Richter scale.

One of the many lessons I have learned is to appreciate nosey neighbours—they miss nothing. Which means you can go off for as long as you like and know that on return, you'll get a full report on who called, when, and a description. I refer to the next-door neighbour Paulette, who is very amusing and typical of village mentality. Her surname is Mme Roqueroll (pronounced rock-'n-roll!), which amused me very much as I conjured up an image of an 84-year-old bopping around to the Beatles!

One Sunday, while sitting out having a coffee and croissant, a man happened to wander by and stopped when he saw the 'for sale' sign I'd put on display, and asked a few questions about the property. However, that particular morning, feeling slightly under the weather, I answered his question politely, using as little energy as was necessary and suggested he could make an appointment to view the following week.

While he stood chatting, I could sense that Paulette's shadowy form was hovering behind her fly screen, and immediately after he left, she pounced—I knew she was dying to find out who he was.

'Was he having breakfast with you?'

No!

'Was he working with Kelvin?' (an ex-pat friend who is involved in the building business). 'Did he want to buy the house?'

Since it was obvious the inquisition wasn't producing anything, she went back indoors and left me to my musings. Shortly afterwards, someone came to the door, and looking around I realised it was her brother, who calls every Sunday morning.

Sometime later I heard him leave and couldn't resist an exaggerated squint in that direction.

Paulette saw me craning round and immediately called out, 'That's my brother!' (in case I might get any ideas about gentleman callers).

Journal Entry, 18 October 2005

This is the ninth day of leaden skies, pouring rain, and nae sun—not even a blink—so I've been creating my own sunshine. I have a number of exciting projects on the go, and this weather is perfect, since it's pouring with rain all the time, going out doesn't feel much of an option. The days are spent, writing, sketching, and dancing (not all at the same time!) to an energetic compilation tape.

I am a naturally friendly, outgoing sort of person, and with my Glasgow-Irish upbringing I have no problem making friends, so life brings me all sorts of encounters and adventures, with a little magic thrown in. These encounters are mostly uplifting. The other day, for example, while writing in the local bar (perfect for this, as the place is normally empty in the mornings), a customer came in sporting a pair of unusual glasses, a cross between goggles and ordinary specs—the difference being the lenses were bright yellow. What's more, I was informed that the lenses were interchangeable with blue ones for sunny days, and they were available from Decathlon Sport's Hypemarket, Bezier. I was invited to try them on and suddenly, the grey day was transformed into a wonderland in *The Wizard of Oz*. Afterwards I realised I was experiencing the difference between perception of reality and *reality* and that we create our own world. So next on the shopping list was a visit to Decathlon to buy a pair of yellow specs.

A few days later I had another encounter, this time with a duck (no, it wasn't wearing specs, just feathers). I could hear the quacking, which seemed to be coming from the bottom of the lane at the end of the street. Sure enough, there it was, wandering round, looking quite lost and possibly finding the weather just too much even for webbed feet. I told it I was on my way. I said I was going to the bakers and would bring back some bread. I set off at a "quacking pace", and in next to no time I was back with a generous off cut from a yesterday's baguette, courtesy of Martine. But alas, the duck had gone.

22 October 2005

Another grey day, but it didn't deter me from my then customary visit to the BioMarché. While waiting at the bus stop situated beside what I'd describe as the grandest house in Creissan, a man came out carrying a black plastic bag, obviously on his way to the pubelle (bin to you). I greeted him as he passed the stop. On his return, he asked me if I lived in the village. This surprised me since I thought my foreign accent was a dead giveaway.

Just before the bus arrived, we managed to have a little chat. He asked about Scotland, and the eternal question came up: "Is there anything worn under the kilt?", to which I gave the standard reply, "No, everything's in perfectly good working order".

When I arrived in Beziers, I went straight to a kiosk to buy a postcard and stamp. While waiting, I overheard the elderly gentleman in front of me ask the assistant for a plastic bag. He was refused this request because his purchase didn't require one (maybe if he'd bought the kiosk, she might have obliged). Now it just so happened I had a whole bag of them with me to give to the woman who runs the vegetable stall, so I offered him one, which he gratefully accepted.

Thought I'd go for a café and croissant and went into a nearby café, only to find they'd run out of croissants. I held my hands, shrugged—and the lights went out!

I passed a remark about the approach of Halloween and spooky things and then left to do some shopping. Later, having bought a croissant from a nearby Boulangerie (could have done that in the first place), I headed back to the first café to have the late *petit dejeuner*. I walked up to the counter, opened my mouth to order—and the lights, having been on when I went in, went out once more and came on again! Magic.

Edin

April 2009

What a chain of coincidences were set in motion when I decided to act on a thought. I have a fallen arch in my left foot, and while in France I had a made-to-measure pair of support insoles, expertly made by Mons Auriach in Narbonne. I had made enquiries in Edinburgh regarding insoles but decided it would be cheaper to go to Narbonne. I could revisit France, see friends, and have a brand new pair of insoles!

After going, and cold on the idea (I hate using the phone), I suddenly decided, why not? I lifted the phone and rang Mons Auriach, who said, of course he could make another pair of *semelles*, but he would need my feet in order to do so! And so it was: booking made, phone call to Susan in the village where I used to live, to tell her of my plan. She was delighted and invited me to stay with the family.

I flew from Edinburgh to Carcassonne, where Susan met me, and we drove to their house, where I spent two nights in Creissan. I had such a lovely time just visiting old haunts. I took the bus to Bezeir, where I bought five Martine books for Paul and had a cafe outside in the sunshine across from Galeria Lafayette.

Forcalquier, Provence

Here I am in Forcalquier, having adventures and coincidences by the minute.

I left Edinburgh on 26 May, bound for Nice, and found myself on a plane full of French students returning after a week in Scotland. Why? Anne Francoise, a friend who had lived in the same village during my stay in France, had asked if I'd like to look after her three cats while she and her partner, Remy, went on holiday.

Nice Airport

It had been arranged that Remy would meet me at the airport. He had seen a photo of me, so at least he had an idea what he was looking for!

Sometime later a man appeared holding a placard with my name on it, so I waved a greeting and he came over to the table where we introduced ourselves. It turned out he'd been waiting at the other terminal! He ordered a coffee and we sat chatting and getting acquainted, and then it was off to find the car and head for Forcalquier.

The journey was around two hours, and we stopped at a

roadside café later, which turned out to be rather amusing. It could be described as an 'upmarket shack', complete with matching waiter and customary fag-end. I had the impression it wasn't frequented by too many travellers, and my vivid imagination conjured a picture of the owner having been called away on urgent business and had enlisted a passer-by to mind the store.

Remy ordered coffee and pastry, but sadly, the pastry man hadn't turned up, so café solo it was. Then about halfway through our cafes, the waiter showed up with a large slice of strawberry tart and asked if we'd like some cream! Yes, of course, and with that, he popped off to the kitchen and brought a large can of spray-on cream, which looked as though it had never seen the light of day until that moment. After a few shakes and presses, out came the cream in a 'splurge', which he liberally sprayed all over the straws. While we polished off the tart, our waiter appeared once more to ask if we'd like some apple pie. Where did all these goodies suddenly come from? Perhaps there was a magic wand in the back ready and waiting for such situations in the absence of the *boulanger*? We thanked him graciously for his offer, paid the bill, and continued the journey to Forcalquier to meet with Anne Francoise.

The first few days were spent catching up on what had been happening in our lives since we last met. The big news of course is the Wedding. Anne and Remy are getting married this August so there is a million and one things to do.

2 June

I had found a little café which had a lovely, cosy atmosphere with a boulangerie right next door. I had come to know the lady in charge and that she spoke English rather well, so on this particular morning, after buying a croissant, I went to the café, ordered a coffee, and sat to relax in the sun and just 'be'.

My relaxation took a different turn, as next thing there was a commotion across the road involving two horses and a foal who seemed to suddenly appear from nowhere. People were milling around French style (lots of hand waving and 'hee-hawing'). I gathered they were trying to find the owner of these beautiful horses. The little foal was so sweet and had special markings in it, which looked as though someone had emptied a bucket of suds on its back. In next to no time this wonderful scenario was played out in the presence of the world and its mother, including the local policeman who arrived, notebook in hand, all business-like. Loud cries of 'Don't touch the foal!' all ended well when the owner was found, thanks to the wonders of the mobile phone.

Of course I wanted to take a photo of this magic moment but remembered the batteries had run out the night before. I sent up a prayer for a miracle, hurried over to the scene, and came away with a first-class photo! Later, after buying some postcards, I went to the post office, and who did I bump into for the third time? Only the woman who had helped me with directions to the flamenco show. We laughed at the coincidence.

I found out there were hot-air balloon flights from the area but understood, on inquiry, that I needed a car to get there. However, one morning, while sitting at a café, I noticed a couple of small people-carrier type vehicles, one with a trailer attached, pull up and park in the square. Nothing unusual in that, you might think, until I realized that I was looking at the high fliers returning from a hot-air balloon trip!

As I watched, the pilot and crew came towards the café and sat at a table a short distance away. Instinct told me to get some info on how I could arrange a flight in a balloon. So I went to their table, apologizing for interrupting the coffee break, and explained why I was there. As luck would have it I found out that the trips left from the very square, so I thanked them and promptly went into the tourist office and booked a flight!

I must say I felt rather apprehensive making my way down to the town centre on a chilly Wednesday morning at six. I arrived to find the other high fliers standing around trying to keep warm. We all shook hands in true French fashion as we waited for our pilot to appear. I could have done with a few more layers but focused on the excitement ahead and the new experience.

The pilot, Philip, turned up, holding a black balloon which he let go into the air (this was to test the wind factor). We all stood gazing at it until it finally disappeared, telling us that conditions were right for flight. We set off for the take-off site, still feeling a bit chilly, me regretting that I hadn't gone to the toilet!

The lift-off site was a large field a short distance outside of town where the balloon was unloaded from the trailer and the slow process of inflating it began. It took twenty-five minutes while we all stood around in anticipation for the signal to get into the basket, which looked rather small to hold fifteen people. We had a good luck message from nature in the form of a little bird which landed on the shoulder of a man in front of me, and then took off!

Then came the big moment when we had to get into the basket, and I confess to having second thoughts about the whole idea when I saw the foot holes in the sides and wondered if I was actually going to get in! I needn't have worried, as there were plenty of hands to give a leg up. When we were all positioned, Philip gave us a few safety instructions, and then it was up, up, and away in this beautiful balloon!

While in the air, the feeling was of no movement and no sound except for the whoosh of the hot air and the sensation of sailing either up or down. Philip took us down to within about ten feet of a lavender field (not yet in flower), and I held my breath as I wondered, *Will we be able to hover?* No worries; everything was perfect. (Well, almost. I have to say, if you ever decide to go ballooning, the basket doesn't leave room for manoeuvring but maybe you don't mind close encounters! Also wrap up warmly.)

The landing was memorable as we were tracked from a van below and guided back safely to earth with hardly a bump. Everyone was expected to help deflate and fold the balloon. I must confess that my help was short lived as I ran out of puff in a very short time and had to retreat and become a spectator. When the balloon was safely packed into the trailer, out came the champagne, fruit juices, croissants, and even a vase of wildflowers that graced the little table. However, champagne is not the best starter to the day on an empty stomach, especially after dropping out of the sky! We were all given a certificate signed by Philip declaring that the holder had gone up in a hot-air balloon and had shown courage and composure. A fitting end to a wonderful holiday experience.

Second Visit to Forcalquier, 30 July

A very testing day. The flight to Nice went smoothly; nothing special, no hitches. The rest of the day made up for that, with a series of blocks and obstacles to give us opportunities to learn.

Anne and Melody came to meet me, and we set off for Forcalquier. We stopped at a café for a drink and a pee. Back into the car and off to a supermarche for food shopping. While driving there was a rattling noise coming from the car and a definite smell of burning, but as luck would have it we were just pulling into the car park and had a chance to investigate the problem. Melody found some pieces of burnt rubber lying inside and around the car.

It was decided to get the shopping done, come back to the car, and make some phone calls. However, there were a few more hurdles to overcome as we discovered when Anne tried to call a garage. The car was dead and needed another battery! Since we were in a shopping area, there was no problem finding a new battery. She rang the garage, where she had to leave a message on an answer phone and wait for a reply. She tried ringing a number of times and eventually someone replied, and she found out that her original message appeared to have gone AWOL. The mechanic eventually arrived with the tow truck, and 'hey, presto!' with Melody seated beside the driver, Anne and I in her car on top of the tow, we set off for the garage, where we were given another car to get us home.

At last, we were on the home straight. Not a chance as there were a few more little problems on the horizon before getting back to base. It was nearly dark by this time Anne discovered the fuel was almost zero. Good news was that we'd just passed a petrol station, so it was a turn around to power up for the last leg of the journey.

Because this was a car on loan, the question arose as to what type of fuel it should take. Anne looked through the usual documents relating to insurance but could find no mention of fuel type. Next on the list was the little problem of removing the fuel cap which, surprise, surprise, refused to budge. We asked a few people who happened to be on the same mission for some help, but nobody was able to unscrew the cap until finally a young man performed the magic by opening the cap and telling us the fuel type, leaving Anne to fill up. At last, voila! We were off!

France

Anne Francoise went to get something called 'chronic installation' (or was it platonic invitation?) last week, for what sounded basically like getting the shit knocked out of her, and what's more, she had to pay for it! Anyhow, when I met up with her, she certainly appeared to be none the worse for the experience and talked enthusiastically of having it done regularly!

I'm actually staying at her house this week, taking care of the cats, keeping an eye on things generally, and having a brilliant time. She's gone to Paris on business and tentatively inquired whether I'd like to holiday at her place. Only one answer to that: Is the Pope Catholic? She lives at the other end of the village in a very spacious three-bedroomed house, complete with a terrace long enough to be continued.

Having a heatwave at the moment (ninety-something a couple of days ago), so life is pretty much on hold; which means basically doing a minimum of everything. I'm surrounded by enough technical wizardry to keep me entertained for a month of Sundays, between two computers (three, if you count my laptop), a music centre that says hello and goodbye, a state-of-the-art TV, to include a video and DVD player, six radios with their bits and pieces to play and record all your music; whew! Add to that the

71

library of books, videos, CDs, and DVDs, and there you have it. A live-in library, office and cinema. I had a feast of Walt Disney-watching classics like *Cinderella, Bambi,* and *Jungle Book.* Just between ourselves, I even sat through a whole double programme of *The Little Prince,* starring Shirley Temple, and a remake of *Heidi.* Now you know why I'm glad I vowed never to grow up.

Since my first invitation to cat sit, I've had two others (on my third at the moment), and the temperature has dropped. Which makes life more comfortable. I was awake at four this morning, got up at five, and went out to the terrace. Brrr … yes, it was very cold and dark, but what a treat to look up into the inky blue sky, filled with twinkling stars and only the sound of silence.

Be Careful What You Ask For!

The house I'm living in at the moment has very small windows (because of the hot weather in summer). One thing I don't like is small windows, and I found myself constantly repeating, 'I want big windows, I want big windows', almost every day. I even became aware of repeating this passionate desire for *big windows,* not only to myself but to friends and family; Then, many months later I had a phone call from my sister, Fran, in Leeds, announcing that eight members of the family had clubbed together to buy a laptop for my very big birthday in March! I had more surprises to follow, but the biggest surprise of all was while practicing with my new toy, I found myself looking at Windows Vista—and had the realization that the universe had granted my request by giving me the biggest windows in the world! Except I'd forgotten to attach a house?

Grizelda

Grizelda walked slowly towards the steps leading up to the platform. The moment she had been dreaming of had arrived. She was about to receive her diploma from the academy where she had been studying.

She felt such joy as she stepped forward to accept the beribboned scroll—when she suddenly tripped on the very last step and fell with a *bump*! She cried out, and when she opened her eyes she was lying on the floor beside her bed.

Alas! It was all a dream. (Grizelda was very good at dreaming.)

She wasn't hurt, but when she caught sight of the clock, she realized it was time to get up for the day ahead. First she had to feed Frijistophene, the cat, and then wash, dress, and have breakfast.

She made her way to the bathroom and made a face at her reflection. Looking back at her was a short, dumpy little figure with a round, moon-like face, teeny-weeny eyes, and a blob for a nose.

You'd be forgiven for thinking she was wearing a bird's nest on her head, but no, her hair was always like that, sort of sticking out and completely unmanageable.

As for the wings—yes, wings—you see, Grizelda was an angel.

'What?' I hear you cry. 'Angels are really beautiful, with snowy white, fluffy wings and—they're perfect!'

Of course it depends on what you regard as perfect, but just as people come in all different shapes and sizes, so do angels.

She may have been a very little angel, but she had a very big dream: to be awarded her diploma and become the personal guardian angel to a little baby on Earth.

What a joy! She began to dance up and down in front of the mirror, clapping and giggling, until she was suddenly aware of the clock chiming and realized she was going to be very late for school if she didn't hurry.

'School? Angels don't go to school!'

Oh yes, they go to school to learn how to become guardian angels so that they can help us when we call on them.

Grizelda attended classes at the Heavenly Academy in Archangel Place. However, there was the little matter of study in order to achieve the diploma, and quite frankly, she wasn't the most academically gifted little soul and had to spend many hours just trying to keep up with classwork. The training included the practice of helping those in need.

Now if there was one thing Grizelda loved to do, it was to be of service to all living creatures. One day, as part of her assignment, she was sent to earth to find and help someone in need. Angels can be anywhere in the blink of an eye, and she found herself on the edge of a wood. Everything was so-oo quiet but for the chirping of the little birds amongst the trees.

Then she caught sight of a little cottage nearby.

'Oh, what a pretty little house', she cried, walking towards the gate.

Just then she heard a faint sound, like a groan, as though coming from someone in pain. She kept listening and walking until she almost tripped over a pile of logs that were strewn all over the ground. It was only then she spied the figure of someone lying on the other side of the little gate.

On closer inspection, she could see this was an old man who appeared to be unconscious, with a nasty-looking bump on his head.

Grizelda immediately produced a little bottle of Miracle Remedy (a sort of heavenly brandy specially for emergencies such as this), applied a few drops to the injury, and the bump simply disappeared. She knew he would recover in a short time, feeling completely refreshed, as though nothing had happened.

She stood back, surveyed the scene, and then went straight to phase two of the helping procedure. She looked around and noticed the doors to a large shed were wide open and suddenly put two and two together.

'Of course, the old man was bringing the logs into his shed when he stumbled and fell! Now I am going to help him by stacking the logs in the shed myself!'

A tall order for such a small angel, but she felt so happy to have this opportunity that she set about the laborious task of moving the logs from the gate to the shed and never stopped until every single log was safely in place.

Naturally she was exhausted after all that hard work, so she found a little grassy corner near the edge of the wood, lay down, and in a trice fell fast asleep, dreaming of her graduation (of course!).

She was just about to receive the diploma when, all of a sudden she was abruptly brought back to earth with the sound of someone shouting in a *very* angry voice.

From where she lay she could see that another man had appeared at the gate and was yelling at the old man, who by this time was wide awake and standing.

'Where in heaven's name did you get to? I've been waiting all morning for the logs I ordered and I arrive here to find they're still in the shed!'

The poor old man was completely mystified and couldn't understand how a pile of logs could have been restacked in his shed when he clearly remembered bringing them out.

He realized that explanations were futile, since his customer's anger was in full flight as he stomped off, leaving behind a heavyhearted woodsman and a guilt-ridden Grizelda, who began to see her assumptions had led her to believe the logs were being brought into the shed instead of taken out.

She applied the first resort for quick-acting aid, otherwise known as 'Divine Intervention', and sent out a plea to the Universal Helpline to resolve the situation to the satisfaction of all.

Almost immediately, the old man heard a voice say, 'Do you have any logs for sale?'

He looked up and saw a young man with a horse and cart standing by the gate.

'Wh-why yes', he replied, thinking he must be dreaming.

'I would like to buy them, please.'

Without further ado, the horse and cart were moved closer to the shed, where, in next to no time, all the logs were loaded, payment made, and goodbyes exchanged, bringing a happy ending for all concerned.

Grizelda sent up a *big* thank you for helping the old man to 'log off', so to speak.

She left the scene a much happier little angel and made her way home to Paradise Row via the local Saintsbury store to do some shopping. There was a special offer on Angel Delight, and since she felt she deserved a little treat, that was added to the basket.

Such was a typical day in the life of Grizelda, and despite any setbacks, she kept the vision of becoming a guardian angel firmly in her heart. She dutifully attended classes and did her best in absolutely everything.

'What an eventful day I've had', she said to Frijistophene the cat, who wasn't in the least bit interested in her day, as there were much more important things in life—such as food, for example. He moved towards the shopping basket.

She lost no time preparing a delicious meal for both of them.

She congratulated herself on having had such a satisfactory day, and as she did the washing up, she began to sing, the signal for Frijistophene to make a quick exit (he couldn't stand this tuneless racket).

After clearing up, she brought out her workbook and prepared to write up her assignment and do some revision for that all-important diploma. She set to with a will to recount the day's events, but alas, she didn't get very far because after a little while, her head began to nod, and then she began to yawn and yawn, until finally—plop!—her head went right down on top of her books.

She sat up with a start and exclaimed, 'I must make some wide-awake tea immediately!'

She poured the tea into a little cup, which had two handles in the shape of wings, then settling herself into her favourite chair, she began to drink—and can you guess? Of course, to dream of that magic moment when she would achieve her heavenly reward, until suddenly her reverie was interrupted by a faint sound.

She thought she must still be dreaming, but no, there it was again, a definite sound coming from outside.

She got up, went to the door, and opened it ve-e-ery slowly. At first she couldn't see anything because it was so dark, but as her eyes adjusted to the inky blackness, she began to make out the form of a tiny child. This totally unexpected apparition rendered our little angel speechless, but only for a moment; it was replaced by an overwhelming sense of love and compassion.

She took the child, who was shivering with cold, inside, and placed it in the comfy chair where, in the light, she could see this was a little boy.

Gone were the thoughts of study, revision, and diplomas, replaced by a sense of urgency to attend to this little creature.

'How could anyone have allowed such a small child to wander around at this time of night?'

She covered him with the softest blanket and proceeded to make some hot chocolate. When all was ready, she sat opposite her little visitor, who sipped gratefully at the delicious hot drink.

There were some questions that had to be answered, and Grizelda suddenly blurted out, 'What is your name, where do you live, and where is your family?'

The child gazed at her with eyes that seemed to enter into her very soul, and he whispered, 'I am the inner child. I have many names; I live everywhere, and my family is everyone.'

Grizelda was completely puzzled by these answers and thought she was still dreaming. She blinked a few times to make sure the child was still there.

'Why did you come to me?' she asked.

'I wanted to talk to you'.

'What about your family? Can't you talk to them?'

'I can talk, but nobody listens', was the reply.

Tears welled up in Grizelda's eyes as her heart filled with compassion at this answer.

The child continued, 'I came here because everyone says you really listen'.

Grizelda moved closer to her little visitor and put her arm around him. She sensed that here was no ordinary child, yet he seemed so down-to-earth and vaguely familiar.

Her thoughts were suddenly interrupted when she realized she was no longer in the room but somewhere out in space, gazing down upon the earth and aware of the child's presence, although she could not see him.

As she watched, the whole shape of the planet became distorted and was spinning erratically out of control! As it spun, she heard a distant sound, which she could only describe as a kind of 'babble', which became louder and louder and *louder*, until she yelled, 'What's happening!'

Back came the reply, 'That's the sound of people talking'.

'But how can they hear what they are saying to each other?'

'They can't, because nobody's listening. They call it the language of communication'.

'That's the craziest thing I ever heard!' Grizelda cried.

She couldn't contain herself any longer and yelled, 'Be quiet!' in such a loud voice, she even startled herself—but it worked!

The babble stopped, and there was no sound, only the sound of silence, the precious sound of silence, until Grizelda's finely tuned sense of hearing detected a faint murmur, which as it grew louder, she recognized as the sound of someone crying.

'Who is crying?' she asked the presence.

'Mother Earth', came back the reply.

'Why is she crying?' was Grizelda's next question.

There was a pause and a very faint voice replied, 'I am sick and need help.'

'What has made Mother Earth sick?'

'This is the result of all the pollution and depletion of Earth's resources.'

'Is that why she is throwing up and has a high temperature?' Grizelda asked.

'Yes', came the reply, 'and this is also being reflected in people's lives in the chaos caused by floods, hurricanes, tornadoes, and abnormal weather patterns'.

'When will Mother get well?'

'When people learn to love, trust, and respect each other and remember why they are on Earth'.

'How can they remember?' was the next question.

'By realizing that all are one and come from the same source'.

Grizelda interrupted, 'And if they don't?'

'They will witness the destruction of this beautiful world and all living things and then see that the perceived reality of materialism—devotion to consumerism, image, and wealth—doesn't exist, because true reality is based on unconditional love, which is the nature of all things. Then they will remember'.

She was about to ask another question when, '*Wham!*' she found herself back in her room thinking she had dreamt the whole thing, because not only was she back home, but there was no sign of the little visitor.

Naturally she felt as though she hadn't slept a wink and simply couldn't stop yawning. But alas, no matter how tired she felt, she knew she must make the effort to attend class if she was to achieve her wonderful dream.

The tutor had a special announcement to make that day concerning the all-important exam. It was to take place the very next week, and all little trainee guardian angels were reminded that they must prepare well by revising.

'I shall spend every single evening studying and nothing is going to stop me!' Grizelda vowed.

So all that week she studied hard, and by the end of it, her poor head was so full, she thought it would burst!

Finally, the night before the exam she surrendered to the

blissful comfort of her cosy little bed, in the knowledge that she had done her very best.

When she awoke the next morning the sun was shining into the room, and a little bird outside the window was chirping, 'Rise and shine, rise and shine, Grizelda. Time to get ready for school!'

She couldn't believe how refreshed and relaxed she felt as she stretched and had a big, big yawn.

'My, what a wonderful sleep I've had!' she remarked as she prepared for the day ahead. Yes, of course she felt some butterflies on her way towards the college, but then, didn't everyone?

On arrival at the gate, she wasted no time and headed straight for the exam hall.

'Why, good morning, Grizelda', a voice behind her said. 'What brings you here today?'

She turned round to find one of the senior angels smiling at her.

'Why, I've come to sit the exam for my guardian angel diploma' she proudly announced.

'I'm afraid that was yesterday.'

'Yesterday! But it can't be', Grizelda cried, trying to fight back the tears. 'I-I just don't understand. I studied so hard all last week, until I could study no more, and then I went to bed last night and—'

'And you slept right through the night before the exam, all that day and last night until this morning. I am so, so sorry, Grizelda'.

With that she put a comforting arm round our little angel

while a stream of tears rolled down the tall angel's cheeks and splashed over her gown.

This wasn't a dream, this was a nightmare!

*

She simply couldn't think anymore and, as if in a trance, she wandered back to her little house, feeling sad and lost.

Just as she reached the gate, she happened to turn round and there, a short distance away, she saw a very old woman who appeared to be looking for something on the ground. Grizelda noticed she was poorly dressed and carried a stick.

The pain of having missed the exam was momentarily forgotten as she moved forward to see if she could help.

'Excuse me, have you lost something?' Grizelda asked.

'Why yes, I've lost my way. Can you help me, please?'

'I live nearby. Why don't you come in for a rest and some tea?'

The old woman gratefully accepted, and as they walked slowly towards the house, Grizelda noticed she was blind.

Once inside, Grizelda busied herself making a large pot of tea served up with angel cakes.

And while they sat sipping the tea, the old woman explained she was trying to find the right path but somehow became confused and had lost her way.

'Where are you going? Perhaps I can help you find the path again'.

'I am looking for the path to love and enlightenment where I will find my true self.'

What in heaven's name was happening? People arriving at

her door wanting her to listen and search for paths! She couldn't understand; after all, she was just a little angel trying to do her best in everything, and she didn't have the answers to all these questions, but her loving heart couldn't refuse anyone.

She looked over at the old woman and tried to think of something helpful and comforting to say—but what? As she sat thinking, a deep sense of compassion welled up inside her, the room was filled with a soft, golden light, and a voice said, 'Look, Grizelda'.

She found she was no longer in her little house but way out in space, looking down upon Earth. She gasped in amazement at the sight of the whole planet, surrounded by glorious multicoloured lights, pulsating with energy, and spinning at a normal rate.

She then began to hear faint sounds, and as they grew louder, she said, 'What's that?'

'That is the sound of all the people of the world communicating with each other through love, peace, and joy.'

'How can this be?' Grizelda cried. 'I thought the world was dying!'

The voice of the presence answered, 'You are looking at the future, my little one, when all nations saw how they were destroying nature and each other with pollution, hate, and wars. They knew they must change in order to save Earth.'

Like before, she was just about to ask another question when she realized she was back in her own little room.

Feeling slightly disorientated, she gradually began to focus on recent events and decided she had been dreaming after all, but what a beautiful dream! Then she remembered the missed exam and felt her spirits plummet.

'My beautiful dream has gone', she whispered, wiping a tear from the corner of her eye.

Just then, she heard a little bird singing outside the window: 'chirrup, chirrup, cheerup, cheerup!'

This made her think of all the wonderful things she had to be cheerful about, and her heart was full of gratitude and she too began to sing.

Her mood changed, and she decided that sitting around wasn't helping, so on that positive note she stepped out into the bright sunshine to go for a walk.

She found herself walking towards the college, still trying to keep her mind free of thoughts connected with the exam.

'I don't really want to go there', she thought, and turned to walk in the opposite direction until the sound of her name being called stopped her in her tracks.

She looked back to see a whole group of angels running towards her, crying, 'There she is, there she is!'

She realised they were the other little student guardian angels from her class. Now, just at that moment, one thing she definitely didn't want was to be faced with anything or anyone connected with the missed exam. So she began to run away!

As the others came nearer, she remembered one of the lessons she had to learn and practise was to accept and face up to all situations—and that's exactly what she did.

She stopped, turned, and stood.

The little group wasn't prepared for such a sudden halt and

almost fell over one another. Then a dazed Grizelda was hugged, kissed, and danced around, while the chant, 'Congratulations!' rang in her ears.

'Stop, stop, what do you mean *congratulations?*'

'Come and see', they cried, as she was almost dragged into the college, down a corridor. and into a room where on the wall were the results of the exam.

'But why have you brought me here?' she cried.

'Look!' everyone pointed to the opposite wall, and there, emblazoned in gold letters, was the name Grizelda. And underneath was printed, 'Special Mention list. Awarded to those who have excelled in the practice of lovingkindness and compassion.'

'But I missed the exam!' she exclaimed.

'You don't need to do any exams', said a voice she recognized as the senior angel who spoke to her on the day she turned up for the exam a day late.

'Assessment, and how you use your knowledge in a practical and helpful way, is an even more important part of your suitability as a guardian angel. Please allow me to congratulate you, Grizelda', said the angel, holding out both hands.

'This is the most special day of my life', she whispered, as everyone around cheered and shared in her joy.

The Graduation

Graduation day dawned. The realization of all her dreams was about to happen.

She had made an extra-special effort to appear at the ceremony looking her very best in a brand-new, snowy-white gown. She noticed that her wings had grown and that her usually unmanageable hair was behaving perfectly.

Standing in front of the mirror for a final check before she set off for the Great Hall of Light, she felt she was seeing the real Grizelda for the first time, instead of always trying to be like others and fit into their image.

'It is my very great pleasure to award this special diploma of guardian angel of distinction to you, Grizelda, for your devotion to the practice of love and compassion towards all living beings, despite your own circumstances'.

Reaching forward to accept her diploma, she realized in that instant that her visitors—the little child, the old woman, the guide, and the Creator—were all one. She felt truly blessed, and her heart overflowed as she returned to her place to thunderous applause and the heavenly sound of the celestial choir.

Now her dream was a reality, and she would soon become a very special guardian angel to a very special little baby born as part of the new generation to bring about the changes in the world leading to love, peace, and joy between all nations.

—M. Connolly, 18 May 2005

The Table

✧

Lucy lived very simply, having only the necessities of life: a little bed, a stove, and a fireplace. There was a small bathroom with a pink bath and a washbasin. The living room had two chairs and a settee a friend had given her. On one wall hung a clock—a rather unusual clock with a big round face, no hands, and no numbers, not even a 'tick'—only the words 'eat when hungry and sleep when tired'.

Illus. for.
THE TABLE

— Lucy & Mons. Claude

People dropped in to see Lucy to exchange ideas and share their problems over a cup of tea and Lucy's delicious scones, and usually left feeling lighter having come up with solutions. Lucy had the gift of listening, which meant that people solved their problems just by talking while she listened. It seems like magic but always worked.

One day a man arrived at her door carrying two large bags of wool. He looked so tired, and his clothes were old and dusty. Lucy invited him in for a cup of tea and something to eat. He was very grateful to be shown such kindness and he sank into the 'big, comfy, welcome chair' with a sigh of relief. She found out he hadn't eaten for days. She made tea and toast served with some homemade jam. He told her his name was Claude and went on to relate his story.

He had been happily married and blessed with a little girl. One day while out walking, his wife and daughter were killed by a speeding car. He was totally devastated and felt his life too had come to an end. After many months, his inner strength returned and he realised he could bring joy to people through his special talent. His mother had taught him to knit using only four fingers. Lucy was amazed as she watched him demonstrate how he could knit a pair of slippers! All he needed was wool, and many people had given him wool so that he could continue to knit little bootees and bonnets to keep up the supply for the demand. Lucy had some oddments of wool, which she gave him and then he set off, refreshed by the tea, toast, and someone to listen to his story.

Who brought the table or where it came from, no one could say, but there it was outside her door one morning. She had thought many times of how she would like a table outside so that people could sit and drink tea on fine days. And here was the answer to her wish. She said thank you to the kind person who had delivered it to her door and set about bringing out the polish and dusters to bring a gleam to its surface. She found the act of polishing very therapeutic and began to sing and smile to herself, grateful for her simple life. Because the weather was fine, she picked wildflowers to put in a vase on the table; then she fed the little birds, made a pot of tea, and sat down to admire the flowers and say another thank you for all the blessings in her life.

The days and months and the changing seasons saw the colours transform to reveal the leaves in their autumn dress before they fell to the ground to create a multicoloured carpet to delight the eyes. As she sat there dreaming, she was aware of a voice speaking softly. At first she thought this was her imagination, but no, there it was again. She looked around, even under the table, until she realized it was the table speaking!

In the story I am about to tell, I sometimes refer to 'we' as well as I and me. You see, I and my family of trees are holograms. Each tiny piece of our bodies, each branch and each leaf, contains the whole. So for practical purposes I will refer to 'I' throughout.

I started life as a very small seed, growing in the middle of a forest far, far away as part of a family of trees. Many years passed, and I grew tall and strong, surrounded by my brothers and sisters. We gave shelter to the birds and little creatures of the forest. How happy we all were, living as part of nature. The sun shone on our branches, the rain washed and refreshed us, and the breeze whispered gently as it passed by.

Sometimes the great wind came, bringing thunder, lightning, and rain to test our strength. This made us bend and stretch, tossing leaves and branches all around. Above all, there was an underlying awareness of the Presence of something which permeated everything and gave the sense of being connected to all that is. This was life before the change.

One day, men came with sharp instruments and axes. They began to chop us down, one by one. We cried but no one heard us. We were separated, cut into logs, and sold to make furniture. I was put together in another form, and one day a farmer came to buy me for his stable, where I was used as a manger for the animals. At first I felt apprehensive, not knowing what would happen in these unfamiliar surroundings. I was put down on the floor of the stable, and a short time later someone came and filled me with hay. Then the animals arrived, jostling with one another to find the best place to eat round the manger. I could feel their warm breath as they began to feed from the hay. I felt so much at home with my new family I didn't want it to end.

Then came the change, and I could feel the energies move.

Late one night a soft light filled the stable, and at one point I felt something being placed in the manger on top of the hay. There were humans gathered round; some were shepherds carrying sheep, others were people from the village as well as my friends who shared the stable. There was a hushed feeling of reverence which remained for many nights.

Time passed, and one day I was lifted from the stable and taken to a carpenter's workshop where I met with some of my brothers and sisters from the forest. Two people worked in the shop, a father and son, cutting and fashioning wood to make tables and chairs and even some little toys.

I was so happy to be among my friends from the forest, feeling so lucky to be in this special environment where there was a deep sense of love and affection. I enjoyed several years there listening to the conversations between father and son and feeling so very much at home while waiting for the next part of my journey and transformation into something to serve.

Then times changed, and the young son left to travel to far-off lands. It was a sad time for us all but especially his parents. And how we missed his laughter throughout each day.

The years and the seasons came and went, until I and some of my family were taken down from the shelves to be made into a large table and transported to an innkeeper's hostel, to be used as a dining table. The rest were left simply as planks, stored to await a future order.

The innkeeper was a kind man, and every day people came to dine and chat over a good meal, such a variety of topics from politics through to everyday family matters and taxes. I heard all these conversations and stored them in my memory. One evening, something special happened, and I was aware of a great Presence in the room. There was a large group around the table (twelve or thirteen) and the atmosphere was filled with the energy of something heavenly. The Presence and power remained with us all.

A few days after that memorable evening, there was a tremendous uproar and sounds of chaos everywhere, which continued for many days, and affected everything around, with vibrations echoing throughout the streets and shaking the very foundations of the building. I was terrified. Then, gradually, it ceased, followed by an uneasy calm. Nobody came to the inn during this time, and I could sense the innkeeper was worried. Then when I thought some element of normality had returned, the skies became black, followed by a fierce storm lasting all that afternoon.

Next day, some people came back little by little, but they seemed subdued, as though their souls had been shaken. It took a long time for life to resume some sort of normality.

I was aware of things changing, until one day the inn was cleared of all the furnishings. I was taken away and put with other items of furniture in a storeroom. I sat there for what seemed a very long time with boxes and chests piled on top of my surface.

Then I heard people talking and discussing the furniture until someone said, 'The most urgent item we need is a table'.

After searching, it was decided there was no table. If only I could speak or call out they would know where to find me! Then, without warning, some of the boxes overbalanced and tumbled to reveal me!

'We only want a small table because of the space available in the ship.'

My heart sank as I knew I was a large dining table. However, when space was cleared to reveal 'the table', everyone gathered round to have a proper look at me. They all agreed this was exactly what was wanted, though I couldn't understand why they would want such a big table. Then I noticed I seemed to have shrunk until I was only one quarter of my original size. How could this have happened? Suffice to say, I was taken downstairs to the street and packed onto a cart along with other goods to be taken to the ship.

I had never seen a ship, let alone travelled in one. The mystery and novelty of it all felt exciting, with endless possibilities in store, so I tried to settle into the journey with an open mind. There were six or seven people on board, including crew members, and we set sail on the evening tide with the most glorious sunset as a backdrop, creating the feeling of a good omen for the long voyage ahead.

My initial excitement soon turned to fear and apprehension when a sudden storm arose during the second night as the ship was tossed round like a cork, bobbing and heaving on the roaring seas while those on board all prayed together. Although the cargo had been secured, the vibration from the force of the storm caused packages to move around, and I slid and collided with contents.

On the second day a light appeared in the sky like a beacon of hope to herald the end of the storm and a return to calm waters. Many prayers of thanksgiving were offered up, life on board gradually settled into the daily routine, and the ship continued to sail on relatively calm seas for what seemed many days. Then land was sighted. Spirits were high at the thought of being in touch with dry land once more.

As we sailed into the port, there were cries to 'Make ready to disembark!' The passengers had gathered their belongings and stood patiently waiting until the ship docked.

We had arrived in Marseille, and I was aware that the people were speaking a different language. I found out later we had arrived in the south of France. This was a great novelty at first, and I felt so happy to think I was with a family once again and would travel with them. Somehow this was not to be the case as I waited to be taken to the cart where my family were loading their belongings. I was separated from them by the chaos caused by so many people all trying to make space for their baggage. I kept being moved and at one time was used to pile packages, boxes, and other things on my surface. Many hours passed when once again I found myself uplifted on to a cart filled with many packages, labelled with names and addresses to be delivered to people in various villages. I was surrounded by packages all bound for a town called Forcalquier.

It was decided to stay overnight in Marseille and make an early start next morning so that the driver and horse would be well rested before the journey.

The next day dawned bright and sunny as the cart set off from Marseille. The journey passed very pleasantly, and we stopped from time to time to deliver parcels. Eventually, when we arrived in Forcalquier, I was taken from the cart along with packages and boxes to the address on the label. The woman who answered the door was very pleased that her parcels had arrived and began to check them. Then she looked puzzled when she came across me because she hadn't bought a table and besides, there was no label on it. She suggested the driver could leave it with her and she would make inquiries among her neighbours. No one claimed the table.

One of her neighbours was Lucy, who had been there for her many times, and who had listened with empathy and compassion during those difficult times in life, always sharing a cup of tea. Lucy had sprung to mind because she knew Lucy had a dream of having a little table to place in the garden, so that more people could come and have tea and a chat.

'And that is how I came to be left at your door, Lucy, to grant your wish'.

Lucy was full of gratitude for the gift and for the wonderful story of the table's life. However, the most exciting part of the whole story was that the table began to grow! At first Lucy didn't notice, and then one morning, just to make sure she wasn't imagining things, she measured it. She measured it the same time next morning, and the next. And yes, it had grown!

More and more people came to chat together and share many things and it was because of the love that the table grew and grew and ...

Well, that's another story.

The Faerie Man

This is the story of Freddie, who worked in a publicity agency, specialising in marketing. Now, Freddie was very good at his job, coming up with original ideas which increased his status in the company. Because of this he was asked to design and present an advertising package for an important new client. Naturally he was very pleased to have been chosen, though apprehensive about the responsibility involved. He was given a month to come up with an original idea and presentation. He threw himself wholeheartedly into the task and worked steadily, with great enthusiasm, buzzing with creative ideas.

When he was satisfied with the finished presentation, he left it aside to switch off completely and put some distance between the work and its creator. A few days later he had a phone call from a friend inviting him to meet at a local bar for a few drinks in two days (the evening before the presentation). This was very tempting considering the intensity of the past three weeks and the fact that he needed some quality time out. So he said yes and met up with Harry at the local bar with the remark, 'Just a couple of beers as I have a busy day tomorrow'.

Well, it's the same old story—a couple of drinks and one for the road until Freddie staggered into the flat in the early hours to find total chaos—the cat chasing what appeared to be a large moth behind the curtain.

Fred fell into bed exhausted and woke next morning feeling like crap. No time for breakfast, so he grabbed the portfolio sitting on the little table by the door and headed for the station. He had to rush to catch the train to work.

He breathed a sigh of relief as he sat back in the compartment. He opened the folder and then dropped it as though it were a hot iron. 'I must have the DTs', he said as he looked into the file to see a small smiling face peering up at him. He snapped the folio firmly and had a quick scan at the other passengers, but they were all stuck in their techno-toys.

He sat back again to try to calm his mind for the rest of the journey. He felt he was on autopilot and didn't actually remember arriving at the agency. He was jolted back into reality when he heard someone say, 'Good morning, Freddie'.

It was Alice, head of reception, smiling broadly and pointing towards the conference room where the presentation was going to take place.

He took a number of slow, deep breaths, made his way towards the table facing what appeared to be a sea of faces anticipating what was about to be revealed. Feeling slightly calmer, Freddie greeted everyone and then picked up page one of the precious project in front of him, glanced at it, and felt the colour drain from his face as he gazed at a collection of tax returns!

Then, without warning, he spoke! He didn't know where the voice was coming from or even what was being said. It was as though someone else was using him to communicate, so he decided to go along with it as he had no other choice.

Finally, he realised there was no voice, only the sound of thunderous applause, colleagues shaking his hand and shouting, 'Bravo!' and 'Congratulations!'

Naturally, at this point he was feeling rather dazed and unable to speak.

As he stood, his mind cleared, and the picture emerged that the project 'he' had presented was something extraordinary and quite original. He thought, 'That's all very well but how can I work on something I haven't even heard?' Strangest of all was the flipchart he was planning to use was covered in designs and instructions. He'd apparently produced all this and didn't remember a thing!

So there it was: ecstatic clients, happy bosses, and an accolade for Fred.

Of course the strange circumstances surrounding his success at the work front were something he kept to himself. Still, he knew there had to be an answer as to how it had all happened—as if by magic, and magic it turned out to be!

One evening, a few days later, while relaxing by the fire, he was aware of a fluttering sound in the room. He turned his head towards the lamp in the corner and yes, that damned moth again. Thank goodness the cat was in the other room. He armed himself with a butterfly net and made straight for the curtain to capture this moth. Moth? As he moved closer, he realised it wasn't a moth, it was a fairy! He sat down with a thump. It was quite clear to him that all the strange things that had happened recently were actually magic!

How could that be? 'That's a load of nonsense!' yelled his logical self. But everything from the 'moth incident'—from picking up the wrong portfolio to seeing the little face peering up at him from inside, and then the presentation—had all come together. What other explanation could there be? He decided to confide in his girlfriend, Molly, and hoped she'd understand and not think he'd gone bats. She said it was all his imagination and suggested he visit a psychiatrist.

He had no other answer and decided to make an appointment with a psychiatrist. He told his story and all the episodes leading up to the discovery that he had a fairy living with him. The psychiatrist didn't freak out and simply took notes and asked a few questions. After the session, the psychiatrist asked him to arrange another appointment at reception.

Seven weeks later it was decided he could resume 'normal' life and appeared to be much more relaxed and looking forward to continuing his work at the agency. He felt so much better as he closed the door after his last appointment.

The psychiatrist sat back in his chair to relax for a few minutes before the next appointment. He happened to glance at the end of his desk where a little face was peering out, smiling from behind a stack of files.

About the Author

Born in Glasgow, 1937. Eldest of a large family. Grew up during the War. Developed an early interest in drawing. Career move led to working as an illustrator in advertising. Other work included painting murals in leisure centres, etc. Has a great love of theatre and realised a dream when she appeared in a play, at the Edinburgh Festival. Loves to travel. Has two sons. Spent three years in San Sebastian with her husband and sons. Now living in Scotland.

Printed and bound by CPI Group (UK) Ltd, Croydon, CR0 4YY